The Little Book of Secret Code Puzzles

*Pearls of Wisdom
& Encouragement
Waiting to be
Discovered*

Gary Ciesla

AuthorHouse™
1663 Liberty Drive
Bloomington, IN 47403
www.authorhouse.com
Phone: 1-800-839-8640

Published by AuthorHouse   04/05/2012

ISBN: 978-1-4685-3212-8 (sc)

Library of Congress Control Number: 2011963058

This book is printed on acid-free paper.

Because of the dynamic nature of the Internet, any web addresses or links contained in this book may have changed since publication and may no longer be valid. The views expressed in this work are solely those of the author and do not necessarily reflect the views of the publisher, and the publisher hereby disclaims any responsibility for them.

Welcome & Introduction

Welcome to The Little Book of Secret Code Puzzles. If you've never solved a Code Puzzle before, or never even heard of a Code Puzzle, you're holding a book in your hands that will bring you a lot of amusement and insight. Some readers, especially those who are experienced puzzle solvers, might say these puzzles are very easy. And they are designed to be easy! But people who have never solved a Code Puzzle before will delight in learning a new skill, after which they'll find that each puzzle they decode will bring them a thought that will humor, encourage, or challenge them.

Each two-page spread contains both a puzzle and a quotation, and each two-page spread of puzzle and quote is related in its sentiment. The quotes come from people who have lived all over the world, and from all ages of history, and each quote gives a clue to help solve the puzzle it accompanies on the opposite page. Some of the puzzles are intended to be a bit humorous, but each contains a little pearl of wisdom that I describe as just waiting to be discovered.

I hope you enjoy solving the twenty-seven puzzles I've included in this book. Most of all, I hope they inspire you! In case you've never solved a Code Puzzle before, I've included a page of instructions just ahead to help you get started. After that, enjoy the challenges you'll find in *The Little Book of Secret Code Puzzles!*

Gary Ciesla
Highland Falls, NY

Acknowledgments

I would like to thank my friend, author Judith Brumbaugh, the President and Founder of the Restoration of the Family, Inc. for her many editorial suggestions. I may have been stubborn, and grumbled at her suggestions, but they were always correct and necessary, and her help has been invaluable! It's also an honor for me to edit her writings, which she posts at http://www.restorationofthefamily.com. I also want to thank my friend Aristide Desvaux for the computer graphics work done as a favor for me. The help was greatly appreciated!

It's also important for me to acknowledge the advice, encouragement, and support that I have received over my entire lifetime from my brothers, Bill Ciesla and Ken Harris. Although we've tangled from time to time, as brothers always do, I think we recognize and appreciate the unbreakable bonds of love and family. We simply must have another Alpha Male weekend, so we can see, once and for all, who's really the Top Dog among us!

I'd like to mention some of the students I taught at the EF International School in Tarrytown, NY during the summer of 2011: Serene, Shucen, Katia, Tak, Carlos, Shahrooz, Yusuf, Marcelo, Naoko, Gonzalo, Michela, Claudia, Daniela, Karina, Wellington, Fabio, Céline, Nadia, Gina, Yuiko, Yuki, Masato, Natália, Silvia, Carmen, Rosália, Seiya, Hiroki, and Marta. (There were also many others.) It thrilled me to watch you eagerly solve these Code Puzzles. I often felt like a chef proudly watching patrons enjoy the meal he prepared for them. I hold great respect for you, as you have worked hard to gain mastery in speaking, writing, and understanding English! Keep up your efforts, and please keep writing to me.

This book is dedicated to the memory of Raymond Ciesla, an uncle who spoke special words of encouragement into my life during a telephone conversation we held in 1974. Little did Ray know the impact of his words would still resonate profoundly within me nearly forty years later. This book is also dedicated to the one still dear to me after sixteen years. My faithfulness to her and to God in honoring my wedding vow continues to be a sacred duty!

Directions for Solving the Code Puzzles

The puzzle sample below is just like the Code Puzzles you'll see in this book. Each puzzle has clues underneath it. In this sample, the first clue indicates that "F is a T." So, underneath every "F" you should write the letter "T". When you do that you'll find that "M" will be an "O," forming the word "TO." When solving the Code Puzzles, look for common letter combinations like this one to help in solving.

The second clue indicates that "L is a B," and it's found in two two-letter words. Those words must be either "BE" or "BY." A Code Puzzle rule is that no letter will ever stand for itself. That means the letter "Y" has to be an "E." After using the clues to fill in as many letters as possible, the puzzle answer is revealed as the Shakespearean quote, "TO BE OR NOT TO BE." One other rule is that the clues go in only one direction. If "A is a B," then "B" will not be an "A."

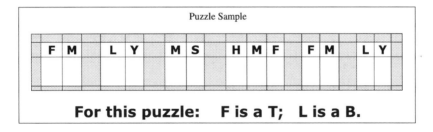

Puzzle Sample

F	M		L	Y		M	S		H	M	F		F	M		L	Y

For this puzzle: F is a T;   L is a B.

The answers to all of the puzzles can be found on pages 59-61 of the book. The Code Puzzle titles are listed in alphabetical order.

**He who has health has hope,
and he who has hope has everything.**

-AN ARABIAN PROVERB

A Priceless Possession

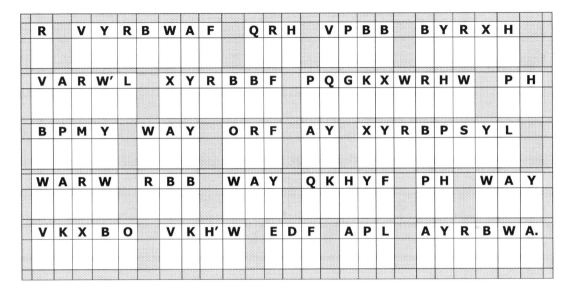

| R | V | Y | R | B | W | A | F | | Q | R | H | | V | P | B | B | | B | Y | R | X | H | |

| V | A | R | W' | L | | X | Y | R | B | B | F | | P | Q | G | K | X | W | R | H | W | | P | H |

| B | P | M | Y | | W | A | Y | | O | R | F | | A | Y | | X | Y | R | B | P | S | Y | L |

| W | A | R | W | | R | B | B | | W | A | Y | | Q | K | H | Y | F | | P | H | | W | A | Y |

| V | K | X | B | O | | V | K | H' | W | | E | D | F | | A | P | L | | A | Y | R | B | W | A. |

For this puzzle: P is an I;   A is an H;   D is a U;   L is an S.

**All truth is good,
but not all truth is good to say.**

-An African proverb

The Wisdom of Our Words

```
G R    P L O    M A L M       P C R L Q B W T    M A R

M Y K M A    B P    L Z G L O P    T V V S.    X K M

P V J R M B    J R P    B M' P    X R M M R Y    W V M

P C V Q R W,    Y R P M B W T    P B Z R W M Z O

B W P B S R    V N    V K Y    A R L Y M P.
```

For this puzzle: M is a T;   R is an E;   S is a D; T is a G; Q is a K.

**The man who masters himself
is delivered from the force
that binds all creatures.**

-Johann Wolfgang Von Goethe

What Does It Really Mean to be Free?

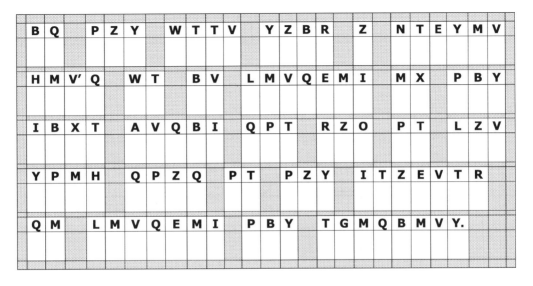

B	Q		P	Z	Y		W	T	T	V		Y	Z	B	R		Z		N	T	E	Y	M	V

B Q   P Z Y   W T T V   Y Z B R   Z   N T E Y M V

H M V' Q   W T   B V   L M V Q E M I   M X   P B Y

I B X T   A V Q B I   Q P T   R Z O   P T   L Z V

Y P M H   Q P Z Q   P T   P Z Y   I T Z E V T R

Q M   L M V Q E M I   P B Y   T G M Q B M V Y.

For this puzzle: Q is a T;   P is an H;   R is a D.

Courage is resistance to fear,
mastery of fear—
not absence of fear.

—MARK TWAIN

The True Test of Our Strength

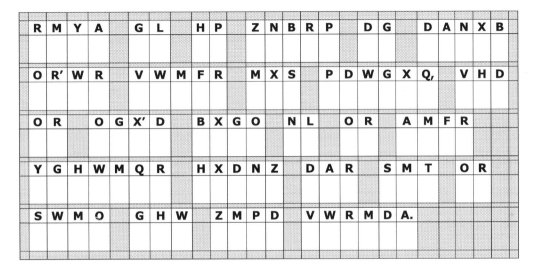

R	M	Y	A		G	L		H	P		Z	N	B	R	P		D	G		D	A	N	X	B
O	R'	W	R		V	W	M	F	R		M	X	S		P	D	W	G	X	Q,		V	H	D
O	R		O	G	X'	D		B	X	G	O		N	L		O	R		A	M	F	R
Y	G	H	W	M	Q	R		H	X	D	N	Z		D	A	R		S	M	T		O	R
S	W	M	O		G	H	W		Z	M	P	D		V	W	R	M	D	A.

For this puzzle: O is a W;   Q is a G;   D is a T;   H is a U.

Ay, sir; to be honest,
as this world goes,
is to be one man
picked out of ten thousand.

-WILLIAM SHAKESPEARE

Honesty Will Give You Courage

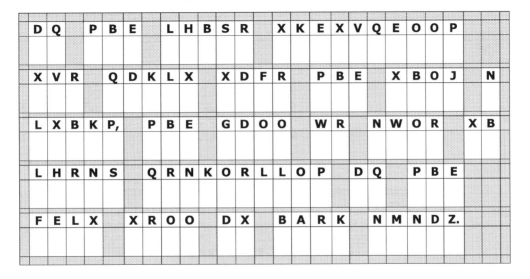

```
D Q    P B E    L H B S R    X K E X V Q E O O P

X V R    Q D K L X    X D F R    P B E    X B O J    N

L X B K P,    P B E    G D O O    W R    N W O R    X B

L H R N S    Q R N K O R L L O P    D Q    P B E

F E L X    X R O O    D X    B A R K    N M N D Z.
```

For this puzzle: X is a T;   D is an I;   K is an R;
W is a B; P is a Y.

I like long walks,
especially when they are taken
by people who annoy me.

-FRED ALLEN

We Can't Please Everybody

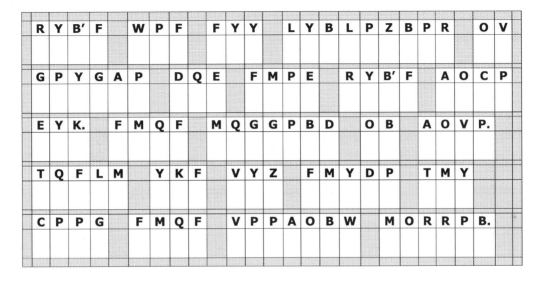

For this puzzle: F is a T;   Q is an A;   A is an L.

Men divide themselves into four classes: (1) Those who never do what they are told —always less; (2) those who will do what they are told—but no more; (3) those who will do things without being told; (4) those who will inspire others and make them do things. It's up to you.

—William J. H. Boetcker

How Do You Measure Success?

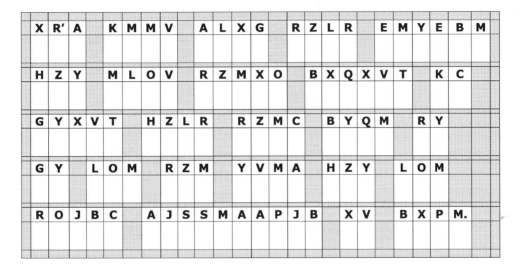

| X | R' | A | | K | M | M | V | | A | L | X | G | | R | Z | L | R | | E | M | Y | E | B | M |

| H | Z | Y | | M | L | O | V | | R | Z | M | X | O | | B | X | Q | X | V | T | | K | C |

| G | Y | X | V | T | | H | Z | L | R | | R | Z | M | C | | B | Y | Q | M | | R | Y |

| G | Y | | L | O | M | | R | Z | M | | Y | V | M | A | | H | Z | Y | | L | O | M |

| R | O | J | B | C | | A | J | S | S | M | A | A | P | J | B | | X | V | | B | X | P | M. |

**For this puzzle: R is a T;   B is an L;   G is a D;
S is a C;   L is an A.**

**Have a purpose in life,
and having it, throw into your work
such strength of mind and muscle
as God has given you.**

-THOMAS CARLYLE

Where Are You Going?

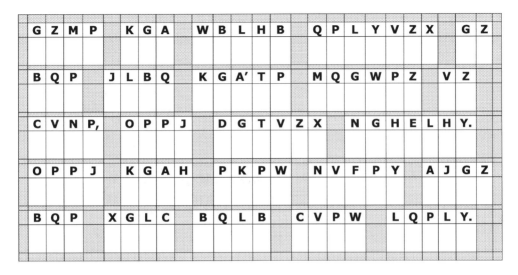

G	Z	M	P		K	G	A		W	B	L	H	B		Q	P	L	Y	V	Z	X		G	Z
B	Q	P		J	L	B	Q		K	G	A'	T	P		M	Q	G	W	P	Z		V	Z
C	V	N	P,		O	P	P	J		D	G	T	V	Z	X		N	G	H	E	L	H	Y.
O	P	P	J		K	G	A	H		P	K	P	W		N	V	F	P	Y		A	J	G	Z
B	Q	P		X	G	L	C		B	Q	L	B		C	V	P	W		L	Q	P	L	Y.

For this puzzle: W is an S; G is an O; L is an A;
O is a K; H is an R.

**The darkest hour in the history of any man
is when he sits down to study
how to get money
without honestly earning it.**

-HORACE GREELEY

The Hidden Actions of the Heart

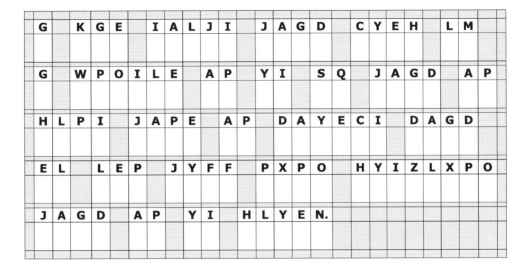

G		K	G	E		I	A	L	J	I		J	A	G	D		C	Y	E	H		L	M
G		W	P	O	I	L	E		A	P		Y	I		S	Q		J	A	G	D		A	P
H	L	P	I		J	A	P	E		A	P		D	A	Y	E	C	I		D	A	G	D
E	L		L	E	P		J	Y	F	F		P	X	P	O		H	Y	I	Z	L	X	P	O
J	A	G	D		A	P		Y	I		H	L	Y	E	N.								

For this puzzle: A is an H;   Y is an I;   M is an F;
J is a W;   N is a G;   S is a B.

21

It's no use going back to yesterday,
because I was a different person then.

-LEWIS CARROLL-

Look Toward What Lies Ahead

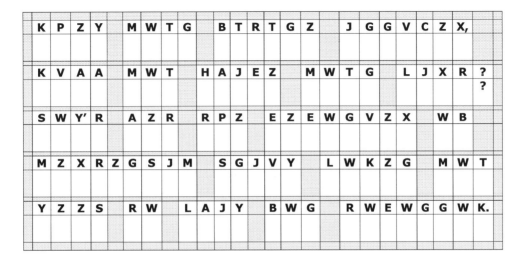

KPZY MWTG BTRTGZ JGGVCZX,

KVAA MWT HAJEZ MWTG LJXR ??

SWY'R AZR RPZ EZEWGVZX WB

MZXRZGSJM SGJVY LWKZG MWT

YZZS RW LAJY BWG RWEWGGWK.

For this puzzle: R is a T;   B is an F;   C is a V;
M is a Y;   V is an I.

Wealth is not only what you have
but it is also what you are.

-Sterling W. Sill-

Finding Out What We're Worth

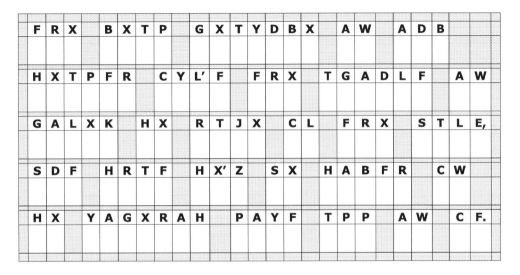

F	R	X		B	X	T	P		G	X	T	Y	D	B	X		A	W		A	D	B	
H	X	T	P	F	R		C	Y	L'	F		F	R	X		T	G	A	D	L	F		A	W
G	A	L	X	K		H	X		R	T	J	X		C	L		F	R	X		S	T	L	E,
S	D	F		H	R	T	F		H	X'	Z		S	X		H	A	B	F	R		C	W
H	X		Y	A	G	X	R	A	H		P	A	Y	F		T	P	P		A	W		C	F.

For this puzzle: H is a W;   C is an I;   T is an A;
L is an N;   W is an F.

**Change is inevitable,
except from a vending machine.**

-AUTHOR UNKNOWN

Are Things Different in the 21st Century?

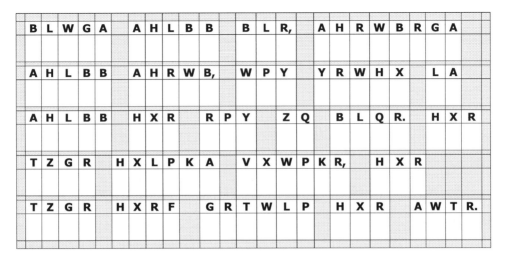

B	L	W	G	A		A	H	L	B	B		B	L	R,		A	H	R	W	B	R	G	A

| A | H | L | B | B | | A | H | R | W | B, | | W | P | Y | | Y | R | W | H | X | | L | A |

| A | H | L | B | B | | H | X | R | | R | P | Y | | Z | Q | | B | L | Q | R. | | H | X | R |

| T | Z | G | R | | H | X | L | P | K | A | | V | X | W | P | K | R, | | H | X | R |

| T | Z | G | R | | H | X | R | F | | G | R | T | W | L | P | | H | X | R | | A | W | T | R. |

For this puzzle: A is an S; H is a T; R is an E; P is an N.

My father asserted that there was no better place to bring up a family than in a rural environment . . . There's something about getting up at 5 A.M., feeding the stock and chickens, and milking a couple of cows before breakfast that gives you a life-long respect for the price of butter and eggs.

—WILLIAM VAUGHN

An Early Riser's Lament

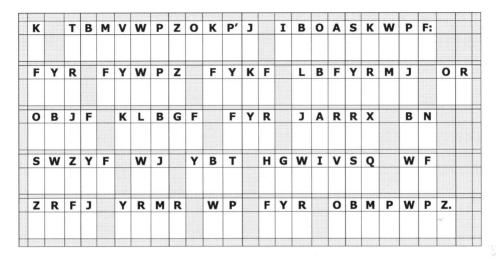

K		T	B	M	V	W	P	Z	O	K	P'	J		I	B	O	A	S	K	W	P	F:
F	Y	R		F	Y	W	P	Z		F	Y	K	F		L	B	F	Y	R	M	J		O	R
O	B	J	F		K	L	B	G	F		F	Y	R		J	A	R	R	X		B	N
S	W	Z	Y	F		W	J		Y	B	T		H	G	W	I	V	S	Q		W	F
Z	R	F	J		Y	R	M	R		W	P		F	Y	R		O	B	M	P	W	P	Z.

For this puzzle: F is a T;   K is an A;   T is a W;
Z is a G;   M is an R.

In the universe,
there are things that are known,
and things that are unknown,
and in between, there are doors.

—WILLIAM BLAKE—

Are There Actions Behind Your Words?

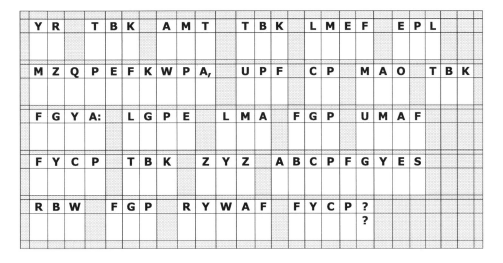

Y	R		T	B	K		A	M	T		T	B	K		L	M	E	F		E	P	L		
M	Z	Q	P	E	F	K	W	P	A,		U	P	F		C	P		M	A	O		T	B	K
F	G	Y	A:		L	G	P	E		L	M	A		F	G	P		U	M	A	F			
F	Y	C	P		T	B	K		Z	Y	Z		A	B	C	P	F	G	Y	E	S			
R	B	W		F	G	P		R	Y	W	A	F		F	Y	C	P	?						
																		?						

For this puzzle: F is a T; P is an E; E is an N; Z is a D; M is an A.

**Greater love hath no man than this,
that a man lay down his life
for his friends.**

Who Can We Count On?

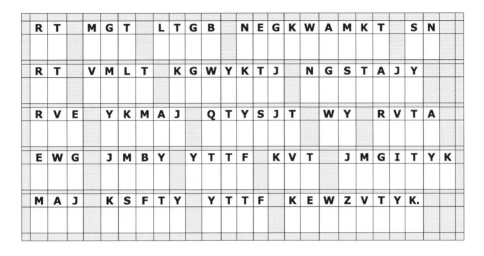

R	T		M	G	T		L	T	G	B		N	E	G	K	W	A	M	K	T		S	N	
R	T		V	M	L	T		K	G	W	Y	K	T	J		N	G	S	T	A	J	Y		
R	V	E		Y	K	M	A	J		Q	T	Y	S	J	T		W	Y		R	V	T	A	
E	W	G		J	M	B	Y		Y	T	T	F		K	V	T		J	M	G	I	T	Y	K
M	A	J		K	S	F	T	Y		Y	T	T	F		K	E	W	Z	V	T	Y	K.		

For this puzzle: R is a W;   N is an F;   E is an O;   G is an R.

A man there was,
and they called him mad;
the more he gave, the more he had.

-JOHN BUNYAN

Gifts That Are Priceless

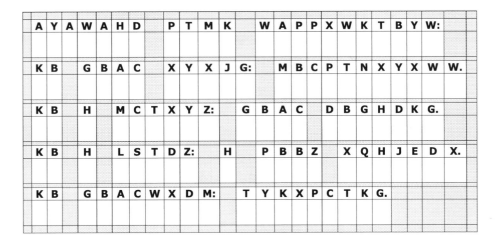

A	Y	A	W	A	H	D		P	T	M	K		W	A	P	P	X	W	K	T	B	Y	W:	
K	B		G	B	A	C		X	Y	X	J	G:		M	B	C	P	T	N	X	Y	X	W	W.
K	B		H		M	C	T	X	Y	Z:		G	B	A	C		D	B	G	H	D	K	G.	
K	B		H		L	S	T	D	Z:		H		P	B	B	Z		X	Q	H	J	E	D	X.
K	B		G	B	A	C	W	X	D	M:		T	Y	K	X	P	C	T	K	G.				

**For this puzzle: X is an E;   A is a U;   M is an F;
K is a T;   P is a G.**

35

Publishing a volume of verse
is like dropping a rose-petal
down the Grand Canyon
and waiting for the echo.

—DONALD MARQUIS

A Poet's Impact

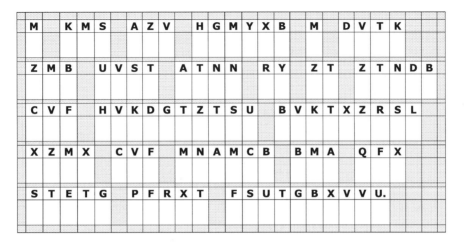

M		K	M	S		A	Z	V		H	G	M	Y	X	B		M		D	V	T	K		
Z	M	B		U	V	S	T		A	T	N	N		R	Y		Z	T		Z	T	N	D	B
C	V	F		H	V	K	D	G	T	Z	T	S	U		B	V	K	T	X	Z	R	S	L	
X	Z	M	X		C	V	F		M	N	A	M	C	B		B	M	A		Q	F	X		
S	T	E	T	G		P	F	R	X	T		F	S	U	T	G	B	X	V	V	U.			

For this puzzle: P is a Q;   R is an I;   L is a G;   Q is a B;   B is an S.

Men are so simple and yield so readily to the wants of the moment that he who will trick will always find another who will suffer himself to be tricked.

—**Niccolo Machiavelli**

Dollars and "Sense"

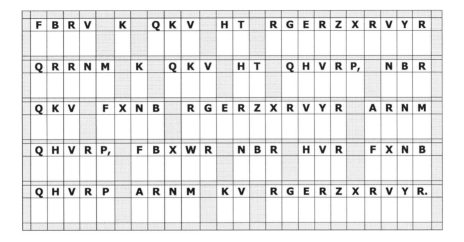

F	B	R	V		K		Q	K	V		H	T		R	G	E	R	Z	X	R	V	Y	R
Q	R	R	N	M		K		Q	K	V		H	T		Q	H	V	R	P,		N	B	R
Q	K	V		F	X	N	B		R	G	E	R	Z	X	R	V	Y	R		A	R	N	M
Q	H	V	R	P,		F	B	X	W	R		N	B	R		H	V	R		F	X	N	B
Q	H	V	R	P		A	R	N	M		K	V		R	G	E	R	Z	X	R	V	Y	R.

For this puzzle: B is an H;   R is an E;   M is an S;
G is an X;   X is an I.

Author's note: The expression used in this Code Puzzle is attributed to Harvey Mackay, author of the New York Times #1 bestseller *Swim With The Sharks Without Being Eaten Alive.*

It is easy to dodge our responsibilities,
but we cannot dodge the consequences
of dodging our responsibilities.

-SIR JOSIAH STAMP-

Talent is Only Half of the Equation

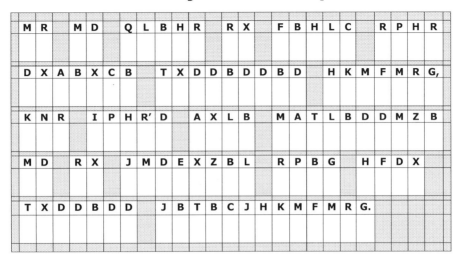

M	R		M	D		Q	L	B	H	R		R	X		F	B	H	L	C		R	P	H	R	
D	X	A	B	X	C	B		T	X	D	D	B	D	D	B	D		H	K	M	F	M	R	G,	
K	N	R		I	P	H	R'	D		A	X	L	B		M	A	T	L	B	D	D	M	Z	B	
M	D		R	X		J	M	D	E	X	Z	B	L		R	P	B	G		H	F	D	X		
T	X	D	D	B	D	D		J	B	T	B	C	J	H	K	M	F	M	R	G.					

For this puzzle: T is a P;   R is a T;   A is an M;
G is a Y;   H is an A.

*The sinister thing about writing
is that it starts off seeming so easy
and ends up being so hard.*

-L. Rust hills

The Voice of Experience

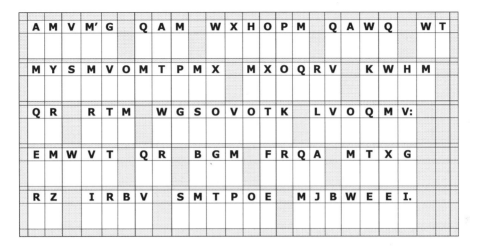

A	M	V	M'	G			Q	A	M			W	X	H	O	P	M			Q	A	W	Q			W	T
M	Y	S	M	V	O	M	T	P	M	X		M	X	O	Q	R	V			K	W	H	M				
Q	R		R	T	M		W	G	S	O	V	O	T	K		L	V	O	Q	M	V:						
E	M	W	V	T		Q	R		B	G	M		F	R	Q	A		M	T	X	G						
R	Z		I	R	B	V		S	M	T	P	O	E		M	J	B	W	E	E	I.						

For this puzzle: Q is a T;   M is an E;   J is a Q;
O is an I;   E is an L.

Dishonesty is a forsaking of permanent for temporary advantage.

-CHRISTIAN BOVÉE

Safeguard the Truth

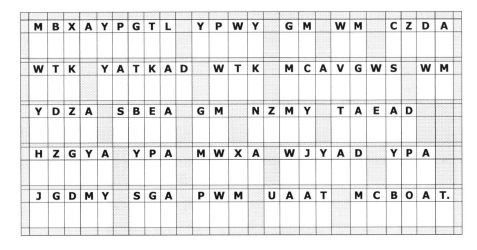

```
M B X A Y P G T L   Y P W Y   G M   W M   C Z D A

W T K   Y A T K A D   W T K   M C A V G W S   W M

Y D Z A   S B E A   G M   N Z M Y   T A E A D

H Z G Y A   Y P A   M W X A   W J Y A D   Y P A

J G D M Y   S G A   P W M   U A A T   M C B O A T.
```

For this puzzle: A is an E; M is an S; G is an I;
D is an R; P is an H.

When I was one-and-twenty
I heard a wise man say,
Give crowns and pounds and guineas
But not your heart away.

—A. E. HOUSMAN

We'll Never Know Why

```
B V O   V O R W B   X L A O B Z A O X   P L O X

Z I Q L A C W O V O I X Z S D O   B V Z I K X

N L W   Z I O T C D Z Q R S D O   W O R X L I X,

R I P   L J W   A Z I P X   E Z D D   I O M O W

S O   R S D O   B L   J I P O W X B R I P   E V G.
```

For this puzzle: B is a T;   V is an H;   J is a U;
Z is an I;   I is an N.

What lies behind us
and what lies before us
are tiny matters
compared with what lies within us.

-OLIVER WENDELL HOLMES

What Do You Think You Are Worth?

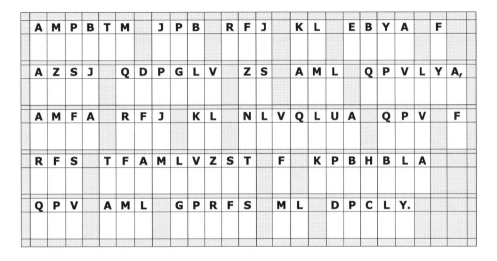

A	M	P	B	T	M		J	P	B		R	F	J		K	L		E	B	Y	A		F	
A	Z	S	J		Q	D	P	G	L	V		Z	S		A	M	L		Q	P	V	L	Y	A,
A	M	F	A		R	F	J		K	L		N	L	V	Q	L	U	A		Q	P	V		F	
R	F	S		T	F	A	M	L	V	Z	S	T		F		K	P	B	H	B	L	A			
Q	P	V		A	M	L		G	P	R	F	S		M	L		D	P	C	L	Y.				

**For this puzzle: M is an H;   Z is an I;   R is an M;
Y is an S;   Q is an F.**

The expectations of life
depend upon diligence;
the mechanic that would perfect his work
must first sharpen his tools.

-CONFUCIUS

Developing Your Talents

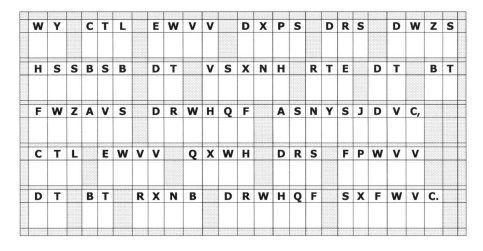

W	Y		C	T	L		E	W	V	V		D	X	P	S		D	R	S		D	W	Z	S
H	S	S	B	S	B		D	T		V	S	X	N	H		R	T	E		D	T		B	T
F	W	Z	A	V	S		D	R	W	H	Q	F		A	S	N	Y	S	J	D	V	C,
C	T	L		E	W	V	V		Q	X	W	H		D	R	S		F	P	W	V	V
D	T		B	T		R	X	N	B		D	R	W	H	Q	F		S	X	F	W	V	C.

For this puzzle: Y is an F;   R is an H;   X is an A;
B is a D;   V is an L.

No horse gets anywhere until he is harnessed. No steam or gas ever drives anything until it is confined. No Niagara is ever turned into light and power until it is tunneled. No life ever grows great until it is focused, dedicated, disciplined.

–HARRY EMERSON FOSDICK, D.D.

Lessons That Last a Lifetime

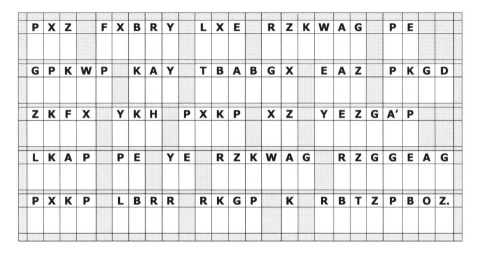

P	X	Z		F	X	B	R	Y		L	X	E		R	Z	K	W	A	G		P	E		
G	P	K	W	P		K	A	Y		T	B	A	B	G	X		E	A	Z		P	K	G	D
Z	K	F	X		Y	K	H		P	X	K	P		X	Z		Y	E	Z	G	A'	P		
L	K	A	P		P	E		Y	E		R	Z	K	W	A	G		R	Z	G	G	E	A	G
P	X	K	P		L	B	R	R		R	K	G	P		K		R	B	T	Z	P	B	O	Z.

For this puzzle: B is an I;   X is an H.

He that gives good advice builds with one hand; he that gives good counsel and example builds with both; but he that gives good admonition and bad example builds with one hand and pulls down with the other.

-FRANCIS BACON

Giving Wise Counsel

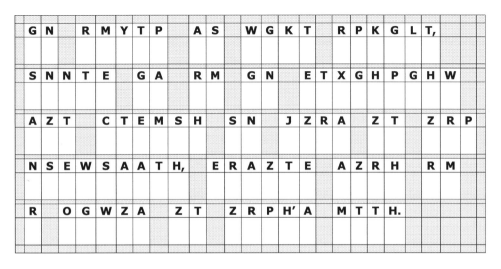

G	N		R	M	Y	T	P		A	S		W	G	K	T		R	P	K	G	L	T,				
S	N	N	T	E		G	A		R	M		G	N		E	T	X	G	H	P	G	H	W			
A	Z	T		C	T	E	M	S	H		S	N		J	Z	R	A		Z	T		Z	R	P		
N	S	E	W	S	A	A	T	H,		E	R	A	Z	T	E		A	Z	R	H		R	M			
R		O	G	W	Z	A		Z	T		Z	R	P	H'	A		M	T	T	H.						

For this puzzle: A is a T;   N is an F.

**Remember not only to say
the right thing in the right place,
but far more difficult still,
to leave unsaid the wrong thing
at the tempting moment.**

-BENJAMIN FRANKLIN

Confidence and Strength Dispel Uncertainty

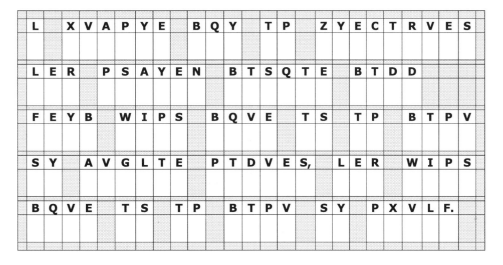

L		X	V	A	P	Y	E		B	Q	Y		T	P		Z	Y	E	C	T	R	V	E	S
L	E	R		P	S	A	Y	E	N		B	T	S	Q	T	E		B	T	D	D			
F	E	Y	B		W	I	P	S		B	Q	V	E		T	S		T	P		B	T	P	V
S	Y		A	V	G	L	T	E		P	T	D	V	E	S,		L	E	R		W	I	P	S
B	Q	V	E		T	S		T	P		B	T	P	V		S	Y		P	X	V	L	F.	

For this puzzle: B is a W;   T is an I;   P is an S;   Y is an O.

For one word a man can be deemed wise,
or for one word he can be deemed foolish.
We should be very careful indeed
with what we say.

THE ANSWERS

TITLES	SOLUTIONS
A Poet's Impact	A man who crafts a poem has done well if he helps you comprehend something that you always saw but never quite understood.
A Priceless Possession	A wealthy man will learn what's really important in life the day he realizes that all the money in the world won't buy his health.
An Early Riser's Lament	A workingman's complaint: The thing that bothers me most about the speed of light is how quickly it gets here in the morning.
Are There Actions Behind Your Words?	If you say you want new adventures, let me ask you this: When was the last time you did something for the first time?
Are Things Different in the 21st Century?	Liars still lie, stealers still steal, and death is still the end of life. The more things change, the more they remain the same.
Confidence and Strength Dispel Uncertainty	A person who is confident and strong within will know just when it is wise to remain silent and just when it is wise to speak.
Developing Your Talents	If you will take the time needed to learn how to do simple things perfectly, you will gain the skill to do hard things easily.
Dollars and "Sense"	When a man of experience meets a man of money, the man with experience gets money, while the one with money gets an experience.
Finding Out What We're Worth	The real measure of our wealth isn't the amount of money we have in the bank, but what we'd be worth if we somehow lost all of it..

THE ANSWERS

TITLES	SOLUTIONS
Gifts That Are Priceless	Unusual gift suggestions: To your enemy: forgiveness. To a friend: your loyalty. To a child: a good example. To yourself: integrity.
Giving Wise Counsel	If asked to give advice, offer it as if reminding the person of what he had forgotten, rather than as a light he hadn't seen.
Honesty Will Give You Courage	If you spoke truthfully the first time you told a story, you will be able to speak fearlessly if you must tell it over again.
How Do You Measure Success?	It's been said that people who earn their living by doing what they love to do are the ones who are truly successful in life.
Lessons That Last a Lifetime	The child who learns to start and finish one task each day that he doesn't want to do learns lessons that will last a lifetime.
Look Toward What Lies Ahead	When your future arrives, will you blame your past? Don't let the memories of yesterday drain power you need to plan for tomorrow.
Safeguard the Truth	Something that is as pure and tender and special as true love is just never quite the same after the first lie has been spoken.
Talent is Only Half of the Equation	It is great to learn that someone possesses ability, but what's more impressive is to discover they also possess dependability.
The Hidden Actions of the Heart	A man shows what kind of a person he is by what he does when he thinks that no one will ever discover what he is doing.

THE ANSWERS

TITLES	SOLUTIONS
The True Test of Our Strength	Each of us likes to think we're brave and strong, but we won't know if we have courage until the day we draw our last breath.
The Voice of Experience	Here's the advice that an experienced editor gave to one aspiring writer: Learn to use both ends of your pencil equally.
The Wisdom of Our Words	We say that speaking the truth is always good. But sometimes it's better not spoken, resting silently inside of our hearts.
We Can't Please Everybody	Don't get too concerned if people say they don't like you. That happens in life. Watch out for those who keep that feeling hidden.
We'll Never Know Why	The heart sometimes does incomprehensible things for inexplicable reasons, and our minds will never be able to understand why.
What Do You Think You Are Worth?	Though you may be just a tiny flower in the forest, that may be perfect for a man gathering a bouquet for the woman he loves.
What Does It Really Mean to be Free?	It has been said a person won't be in control of his life until the day he can show that he has learned to control his emotions.
Where Are You Going?	Once you start heading on the path you've chosen in life, keep moving forward. Keep your eyes fixed upon the goal that lies ahead.
Who Can We Count On?	We are very fortunate if we have trusted friends who stand beside us when our days seem the darkest and times seem toughest.

About the Author

Gary Ciesla is a writer and a veteran teacher who has worked in a variety of interesting and challenging classroom environments. He has taught in state and federal prisons, in institutions for troubled youth, and most recently, at EF International in Tarrytown, New York, where he first taught English to students from around the world, and then managed the EF/NY University Pathways Program.

As an author, Mr. Ciesla has written and published *The Logic Puzzle Project*. He is a member of the American Cryptogram Association, and currently lives in Highland Falls, New York.

Mr. Ciesla can be reached, via email, at the following address: *gary.ciesla@gmail.com*

Here's what others have said about
The Little Book of Secret Code Puzzles:

"*The Little Book of Secret Code Puzzles* is a charming book full of cleverly designed sentence puzzles that teach values while challenging the mind. It is a fantastic book to teach advanced thinking and reasoning skills and a wonderful source to help adults, young and old, keep their minds active and alert in truly an enjoyable manner. *The Little Book of Secret Code Puzzles* is truly a real gem!"

Addie Cusimano, M.ED. Reading specialist, diagnostician and clinician, and author of *Learning Disabilities: There is a Cure* as well as numerous teaching materials for the development of specific learning skills. www.achievepublications.com

****

"Many thanks to Gary Ciesla for creating this book. What a great idea! The book presents a fine collection of inspirational quotations and readers who decode the messages learn an excellent problem solving skill. The puzzles appeal to a wide range of students. They create enthusiasm and a sense of accomplishment. Hats off to Ciesla for a book that generates excitement and teaches a valuable problem solving skill."

-Gregg Young, author of *Reasoning Backward: How Sherlock Holmes Can Make You a Better Problem Solver* ISBN-13: 978-0-9830113-0-9 www.youngassocinc.com

"To understand why things go right, observe what's different when things go wrong."

****

"A True Treasure! This puzzle book is a shear gem, filled will easy to solve quotes worth remembering. I expect to see this book in nursing homes and doctor's offices as well as special ed. schools."

Ginger Marks, CEO DocUmeant Designs www.DocUmeantDesigns.com

Here's what others have said about
The Little Book of Secret Code Puzzles (continued):

****

"Remember when you were a child and you along with a very small, exclusive group of your friends created your own secret code? You shared the privilege and excitement of only the very, small group of you being absolutely in the know. Can't you just feel right now how it felt when you all agreed on what the secret code was and how creative you all were? Gary Ciesla, author of The Little Book of Secret Code Puzzles has created an opportunity for you to experience those feelings again. I heartily encourage you to discover the pearls of wisdom and encouragement he has included in the book through the wonder of secret code puzzles. Unlike when you were a child, these are not secrets you will want to keep!"

-Gary Greenfield, author of *Life's Ride or Fall . . . You Make the Call. Thoughts, Stories, Lessons Learned and Actionable Ideas to Help Create the Ride of Your Life!*
www.garygreenfield.com Twitter: LifeRider

****

I found this book to be not only very interesting, but also educational, especially for foreign students trying to learn English. It would definitely make the learning process more fun for them, and will stimulate them to learn more. I also like the fact that, should you decide to have future editions, which I hope you will, you could tailor them to various levels of difficulty for the benefit of a wider group of readers. Thank you for writing this book, and thank you for allowing me to contribute my comments.

Reza Mashayekhi, author of *English Idioms And Expressions For Everyone, Yes, Even You!* www. *English-Idioms-And-Expressions.com*

PLEASE TAKE A MOMENT TO VISIT THE AUTHOR'S WEBSITE

AlaraLearning.com

ALARA Learning
Arithmetic, Language & Reading Activities

At AlaraLearning.com you will find:

- Lots of free samples of great classroom-tested materials for teachers of Arithmetic, Language Arts, and Reading.

- A wide selection of materials for Special Education and ESL teachers to immediately use with students in their classrooms.

- Scores of PDF's of Code Puzzles, Logic Puzzles, Word Puzzles, Math Puzzles, Language Puzzles (and more!) all at unbelievable prices and with the right to photocopy included with each PDF purchased!

- A link to the interactive app for *The Little Book of Secret Code Puzzles*, now available for download onto devices that support the Android platform (Kindle Fire, Nook, etc.) and sold at a very reasonable price.

ALARA Learning

A different kind of company, that's for sure!